M000012310

WORLD'S GREATEST

DAD JOKES

192

MORE

HILARIOUS
KNEE-SLAPPERS
AND
HOKEY PUNS

World's Greatest Dad Jokes, Volume 2

13-Digit ISBN: 978-1-60433-902-4
10-Digit ISBN: 1-60433-902-0

This book may be ordered by mail from the publisher. Please include $5.99 for
postage and handling. Please support your local bookseller first!
Books published by Cider Mill Press Book Publishers are available at special
discounts for bulk purchases in the United States by corporations, institutions,
and other organizations. For more information, please contact the publisher.

Cider Mill Press Book Publishers
"Where good books are ready for press"
PO Box 454
12 Spring Street
Kennebunkport, Maine 04046
Visit us online!
cidermillpress.com

Typography: Adobe Garamond, BodoniFB, Clarendon,
Futura, Hanley Sans, Helvetica, Industry Inc.

Printed in China
1 2 3 4 5 6 7 8 9 0
First Edition

WORLD'S GREATEST

DAD JOKES

192

MORE

HILARIOUS
KNEE-SLAPPERS
AND
HOKEY PUNS

CIDER MILL PRESS

BOOK PUBLISHERS
KENNEBUNKPORT, MAINE

Contents

Introduction

Dad Jokes are a staple of punsters and jokesters everywhere, from bona fide dads to faux pa hipsters looking for the next big thing. Anyone can tell a Dad Joke, but it takes a true master to own a Dad Joke.

Some people argue that puns and wordplay are the lowest forms of humor, and while there's no one lining up to hand out Oscars for Best Dad Joke (we'd be first in the running if that were the case), there is a time-honored art to crafting a punch line that will leave your audience groaning in begrudging admiration.

You don't have to be a dad to tell a Dad Joke, but you do need to have the heart and soul of a dad to truly embody the spirit of the Dad Joke. You need to let any embarrassment you may feel go to the wind, along with your true comedy credentials. Embrace the wordplay, twist those homophones as far as they can go, and take on the mantle of World's Greatest Dad Joker.

Developing your own Dad Jokes takes time, and frankly, a lot of effort. And while you may be equipped to toss out the perfect "Does your face hurt? It's killing me!" every once and a while, your witty comebacks may start to run dry halfway through your next family BBQ. And who would want that to happen?

Study this handbook, become this handbook, and let the Tao of Dad be your guide. You can use these jokes as an emergency stock for those less-than-dad-like days where you just can't seem to think of a play on words about camping (the pressure can be so in tents), or use them to inspire your joke de résistance.

Or, if you're not a fan of the exalted Dad Joke, you can use this book as Dad Joke Kryptonite. Study the punch lines, learn the wordplay techniques, but be warned: the process of truly defeating Dad Jokes requires you to become a Dad Joke master.

So whether you're looking to take your Dad Joke skills to the top of the proverbial charts or want to cut off potential bad puns at the knees, this book is stocked with dozens and dozens of our best Dad Jokes, from historical jabs (sorry Caesar) to cheesy cheese jokes, meaning you'll never again find yourself in short supply of goofy zingers.

So dust off your mic, give the begrudging audience your best smile, and get ready to have the last (and only) laugh with these terribly perfect Dad Jokes.

1.

DID YOU HEAR . . . ?

Did you hear about the tense mummy?

He was all wound up.

Did you hear about the mummy with back problems?

He went to a Cairo-practor.

Did you hear why Medusa broke up with her boyfriend?

He was always stoned.

Did you hear about the centurion who got lost?

HE WAS JUST ROMAN AROUND.

....

Did you hear about the Boston silversmith?

PEOPLE REALLY REVERE HIM.

Did you hear about the janitors who went to space?

They had to scrub the mission.

Did you hear about the napping car?

I guess it was tired.

Did you hear about the housekeeper who was arrested?

SHE WAS LAUNDERING MONEY.

Did you hear about the gymnast who filled out paperwork?

SHE HAD A PERFECT FORM.

DID YOU HEAR ABOUT THE FOOTBALL PLAYER WHO GOT ARRESTED?

He really needs to work on his defense.

Did you hear about the frog who double parked?

HE GOT TOAD.

Did you hear about the car that climbs mountains?

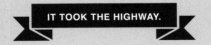

IT TOOK THE HIGHWAY.

Did you hear the joke about the equation?

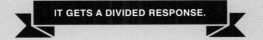

IT GETS A DIVIDED RESPONSE.

....

Did you hear about the ice thief that got away?

HE WAS TOO SLICK.

Did you hear about the skeleton who thought the world was flat?

He was dead wrong.

Did you hear they made round bales of hay illegal in Wisconsin?

It's because the cows weren't getting a square meal.

Did you hear about the ice salesman?

They say he's cracked.

Did you hear about the cheese salesman?

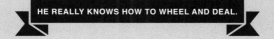

HE REALLY KNOWS HOW TO WHEEL AND DEAL.

....

Did you hear about the new blizzard trend?

IT'S TAKING THE WORLD BY STORM.

DID YOU HEAR ABOUT THE MORTICIAN WORKING OVERTIME?

He was dying to leave.

Did you hear about the zombie baker?

The pastries are to die for!

Did you hear about the French cheese factory that exploded?

THERE WAS NOTHING LEFT BUT DE BRIE.

Did you hear about the actor who fell through the floorboards?

HE WAS JUST GOING THROUGH A STAGE.

Did you hear about the ATM that was addicted to money?

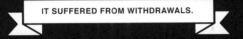

IT SUFFERED FROM WITHDRAWALS.

Did you hear about the man who fell into an upholstery machine?

HE'S FULLY RECOVERED.

Did you hear about that new band 923MB?

They're good but they haven't got a gig yet.

Did you hear about the music group called Cellophane?

They mostly wrap.

2.

WHY ...?

Why did the bull fail his driver's test?

He kept laying on the horn.

Why couldn't the banana find a date?

No one found him apeeling.

Why did the banana leave the party early?

He had to split.

Why did the Romans hate Cleopatra?

She was a bit of an asp.

Why aren't Greeks morning people?

BECAUSE DAWN IS TOUGH ON GREECE.

Why did the drowning pharaoh refuse to ask for help?

HE WAS IN DE NILE.

WHY DID THE GREEK GODDESS GET A PARKING TICKET?

Demeter wasn't working.

WHY DID THE ROBBER GIVE THE MONKEY BACK HIS WALLET?

He wasn't in it for chimp change.

....

WHY DID THE GORILLA GO SEARCHING FOR BURIED TREASURE?

He wanted his silverback.

WHY DID THE ATHLETE GO TO GREECE?

He wanted to visit the Temple of Nike.

....

WHY WOULD PROMETHEUS MAKE A GOOD MAILMAN?

It's a job with a lot of de-livering.

Why was emo music popular in Rome?

The Goths invaded.

Why was Julius Caesar afraid to go to the DMV in the spring?

He was told to beware the IDs of March.

Why is it hard to win an argument with a Roman?

If you're not forum you're against 'em.

Why couldn't Mark Antony use his cell phone?

Because he was on Roman data.

Why was the
Liberty Tree
cut down?

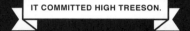

IT COMMITTED HIGH TREESON.

Why was the explorer
so bad at basketball?

HE WAS ALWAYS TRAVELING.

WHY WAS THE BASKETBALL PLAYER BAD AT FISHING?

He got nothing but net.

Why did the soccer player go to the bar?

He had no goals.

Why was the poker player arrested?

He started dealing.

Why did the announcer say "Touchdown!" when he was angry?

Because someone crossed a line.

Why did the law student take a different road home?

He wanted to pass the bar.

Why should you never shop at a notebook store?

There are too many lines.

Why did the pirates pay for extra luggage?

They had a stowaway.

Why was the pilot fired?

HE COULDN'T MAKE DECISIONS ON THE FLY.

Why was the math book in therapy?

BECAUSE IT HAD SO MANY PROBLEMS.

Why did the melting snowman cover himself in pickles?

HE WANTED TO BE COOL AS A CUCUMBER.

....

Why can't you find parking in Alaska?

THERE'S SNOW MORE ROOM.

WHY DID THE CHEMIST JOIN A DATING SITE?

He got lonely periodically.

....

WHY WAS THE CHEMISTRY DEPARTMENT LOSING SECRETS?

They couldn't find the mole.

WHY DID THE SCIENTIST START A CHURCH?

He was great at conversions.

....

WHY DID THE SEISMOGRAPH QUIT HIS JOB?

He wasn't ready for a position of that magnitude.

Why was the analyst mad about getting free food?

HE DIDN'T LIKE THE SAMPLE SIZE.

Why does a giant always apologize first?

HE'S THE BIGGER PERSON.

Why did the mozzarella get away with murder?

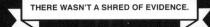
THERE WASN'T A SHRED OF EVIDENCE.

Why couldn't the cheese go swimming?

THE WATER WAS WHEY TOO DEEP.

Why did the Swiss cheese become a priest?

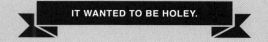

IT WANTED TO BE HOLEY.

Why should you never whisper around Parmesan?

IT TRIES TO WEDGE ITS WAY INTO THE CONVERSATION.

Why did the skeleton buy cough syrup?

HE COULDN'T STOP COFFIN.

··

Why did the octopus beat the shark in a fight?

BECAUSE IT WAS WELL ARMED.

Why don't seagulls fly over the bay?

Because then they'd be bay-gulls.

Why did the man name his dogs Rolex and Timex?

Because they were watch dogs.

WHY ARE THERE NO GOOD JOKES ABOUT DOGS?

They're all a little far-fetched.

Why don't cows wear flip-flops?

They lactose.

Why do bees stay in their hive during the winter?

Swarm in there.

Why do chicken coops only have two doors?

Because if they had four, they would be chicken sedans.

Why did the singer bring a bucket with him when he performed?

To help him carry the tune.

Why was the teacher cross-eyed?

Because he couldn't control his pupils.

Why did the period break up with the apostrophe?

It was too possessive.

WHY DID THE SITCOM ABOUT AIRPLANES NEVER TAKE OFF?

The pilot was terrible.

WHY SHOULD YOU NEVER TRUST A FISHERMAN?

They're always angling for something.

Why doesn't Oedipus swear?

HE KISSES HIS MOTHER WITH THAT MOUTH.

Why did the coffee file a police report?

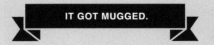

IT GOT MUGGED.

Why did the cookie cry?

BECAUSE HIS FATHER WAS A WAFER SO LONG.

Why should you never take driving directions from a life coach?

THEY KEEP TELLING YOU TO GO THE EXTRA MILE.

3.

WHAT . . . ?

WHAT DO YOU CALL A CHIMP WITH A BAD SPRAY TAN?

Orangutan.

What do you call it when a mummy charges you too much?

Egypt'd you!

What did the pharaoh's mother say when she was disappointed?

"Tut, tut..."

What do you call an ancient Egyptian?

An old Giza.

What's red, purple, and full of knives?

Julius Caesar.

What do you call a Roman leader putting on clothes?

Caesar dressing.

What's the difference between a duck and George Washington?

One has a bill on his face, the other has his face on a bill.

What's a patriot's least favorite breakfast?

Eggs Benedict Arnold.

WHAT DID THE AMERICAN SEE AFTER HE GOT KNOCKED OUT?

Stars and stripes forever.

. . . .

WHAT DO MUSKETS DO IN THE BATHROOM?

They powder their noses.

WHAT DO YOU CALL THE VICE PRESIDENT IN WINTER?

Aaron Burr.

....

WHAT DID THE POLICEMAN SAY TO THE MUSICAL NOTE?

"You're under a rest!"

WHAT DO YOU CALL A BALD PRISONER?

A smooth criminal.

What birds fly to Lisbon for the winter?

PORTUGULLS.

What did the cosmonaut say when he was running late for work?

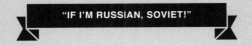

"IF I'M RUSSIAN, SOVIET!"

WHAT DO YOU CALL A NUMBER THAT CAN'T SIT STILL?

A Roman numeral.

What does a mathematician use to clean their house?

Cleaning solution.

What do snowmen do in their spare time?

Just chill.

What do you do with a sick chemist?

If you can't helium, and you can't curium, then you might as well barium.

WHAT DO YOU CALL THE PLACE WHERE A BRITISH SCIENTIST WORKS?

A lab for a Tory.

What is Peter Pan's favorite restaurant?

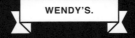

WENDY'S.

What did the Three Little Pigs say when they quit their job?

"THIS IS THE LAST STRAW!"

What did the tomatoes say to the cucumbers?

"LETTUCE INTRODUCE OURSELVES."

What did the cooking cheese say to the wicked witch?

"I'M MELTING!"

What did the haunted house owner say to the enthusiastic ghost hunter?

"That's the spirit!"

What do you call a fake noodle?

An Impasta.

What do you call an elephant that doesn't matter?

An irrelephant.

What did the grape do when he got stepped on?

He let out a little wine.

What do you call a belt with a watch on it?

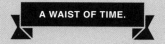

A WAIST OF TIME.

···

What do you call a man with no nose and no body?

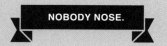

NOBODY NOSE.

What do you call a group of killer whales playing instruments?

AN ORCA-STRA.

What do you call a dog that can do magic?

A LABRACADABRADOR.

What is Beethoven's favorite fruit?

A ba-na-na-na.

What did the horse say after it tripped?

"Help! I've fallen and I can't giddyup!"

WHAT DO YOU GET WHEN YOU CROSS A SNOWMAN WITH A VAMPIRE?

Frostbite.

What does an angry pepper do?

It gets jalapeño your face.

What do you call a fish with two knees?

A "two-knee" fish.

What do you call it when prisoners take their own mug shots?

Cellfies.

What did the officer molecule say to the suspect molecule?

I've got my ion you.

What lies at the bottom of the ocean and twitches?

A nervous wreck.

What do you call a snowman with a six-pack?

An abdominal snowman.

What do you call an explosive horse?

Neigh-palm.

What do you call a horse that moves around a lot?

Unstable.

What's the difference between a poorly dressed man on a tricycle and a well-dressed man on a bicycle?

Attire!

What do you call a dinosaur that crashes his car?

TYRANNOSAURUS WRECKS.

....

What do you call a pile of cats?

A MEOW-TAIN.

What do you call a million rabbits walking backward?

A RECEDING HARELINE.

What do you call it when someone who doesn't have any kids makes a Dad Joke?

A FAUX PA.

What's a foot long and slippery?

A SLIPPER.

What do you call it when the letter A uses the bathroom?

A VOWEL MOVEMENT.

What do you call a fish with no eyes?

A FSH.

Why did the Little Mermaid need singing lessons?

SHE ALWAYS SANG UNDER THE C.

What does a house wear to a party?

Address.

What do you call someone who has ten ants?

A landlord.

4.

PERSONAL
ANECDOTES

I USED TO BE ADDICTED TO SOAP, BUT NOW I'M CLEAN.

I USED TO MAKE MONEY REMOVING PAINT.

Now I barely scrape by.

I met an astronaut but we haven't seen each other since.

I guess we travel in different orbits.

I applied for a job as an archaeologist.

I could see myself really digging the job.

I couldn't find parking at the library convention.

It was overbooked.

I heard there's a secret club at the library.

It's very hush-hush.

I played a strategy game with my math book.

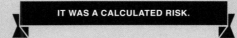

IT WAS A CALCULATED RISK.

....

I don't think I could become a sniper.

NOT BY A LONG SHOT.

I tried to
introduce myself
to a snowman,
but he gave
me the cold
shoulder.

I HAD A JOB INTERVIEW AT A CONSTRUCTION SITE.

Nailed it.

....

NEVER BELIEVE WHAT THE BIG BAD WOLF TELLS YOU.

He's a real blowhard.

I USED TO BE OBSESSED WITH VEGETABLES.

Now I don't carrot all.

....

I USED TO WORK AS A CHEESE TASTER, BUT I DIDN'T THINK IT WAS A GOUDA-NOUGH CAREER FOR ME.

I hear there's a tuna thief in town.

Seems fishy to me...

I heard a rumor about the town dump.

But it's a load of garbage.

I was diagnosed as colorblind.

It really came out of the purple.

Last night I dreamt I was a muffler.

I woke up exhausted.

I was interrogated over
the theft of a panini.

MAN, THEY REALLY GRILLED ME.

I always get
nostalgic when I put
my car in reverse.

IT REALLY TAKES ME BACK.

I swapped my bed for a trampoline.

My wife hit the roof.

I HAVE A FEAR OF SPEED BUMPS BUT I'M SLOWLY GETTING OVER IT.

I asked my date to meet me at the gym, but she never showed up.

I guess we'll never work out.

I've been telling everyone about the benefits of eating dried grapes.

I'm all about raisin awareness.

I just found out my friend has a secret life as a priest.

It's his altar ego.

I stopped ironing my clothes.

I've got more pressing concerns.

I can cut wood just by looking at it.

It's true! I saw it with my own eyes!

MY BALD SURGEON IS THE MOST CHARISMATIC MAN I'VE EVER MET.

He's a real smooth operator.

My archaeologist friend has been depressed lately.

HIS LIFE IS REALLY IN RUINS.

My wife refuses to go to karaoke with me.

I HAVE TO DUET ALONE.

MY WIFE IS ON A TROPICAL FOOD DIET.

It's enough to make a mango crazy.

....

MY LACK OF KNOWLEDGE ABOUT GREEK MYTHOLOGY WILL ALWAYS BE MY ACHILLES' ELBOW.

NO ONE LAUGHED AT MY JOKE ABOUT OUTER SPACE.

I guess it wasn't a universal experience.

....

I HEARD A JOKE ABOUT THE AMERICAN REVOLUTION.

They really tea-d up the punch line.

I'm writing a joke about a builder.

I still have to hammer out some of the details.

I used to tell a lot of science jokes.

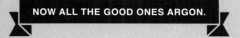

NOW ALL THE GOOD ONES ARGON.

I heard a new joke about Goldilocks.

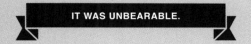

IT WAS UNBEARABLE.

I hate jokes about German sausages.

They're the wurst.

I tried to come up with jokes about golf, but they were all subpar.

5.

JOKE OF ALL
TRADES

HOW MANY EARS DOES CAPTAIN KIRK HAVE?

The left ear, the right ear, and the final frontier.

....

HOW DID THE APE BECOME A CEO?

He climbed the corporate ladder.

HOW DO EGYPTIAN ANTS COMMUNICATE?

With pharaohmones.

....

HOW DO GREEK WOMEN GET READY FOR A TOGA PARTY?

With a Hera appointment.

How does Norway keep track of their warships?

They Scandinavian.

How can you tell when a horse is sad?

He has a long face.

How do tectonic plates apologize?

"My fault!"

How many apples grow on a tree?

ALL OF THEM.

How much does a hipster weigh?

AN INSTAGRAM.

Where do cows go on dates?

THE MOOVIES.

Where does the king of the monkeys live?

THE REIGN FOREST.

Where do you learn to make ice cream?

Sundae school.

Where can you buy chicken broth in bulk?

The stock market.

When do zombies work?

The graveyard shift.

TWO GOLDFISH
ARE IN A TANK. ONE
SAYS TO THE OTHER,
"DO YOU KNOW HOW TO
DRIVE THIS THING?"

....

TWO GUYS WALK
INTO A BAR, THE
THIRD ONE DUCKS.

A MIME WAS ARRESTED AFTER GETTING INTO A BAR FIGHT AND BREAKING HIS LEFT ARM.

He still has the right to remain silent.

....

MOUNTAINS AREN'T JUST FUNNY.

They're hill areas.

About Cider Mill Press Book Publishers

Good ideas ripen with time. From seed to harvest, Cider Mill
Press brings fine reading, information, and entertainment
together between the covers of its creatively crafted books.
Our Cider Mill bears fruit twice a year, publishing
a new crop of titles each spring and fall.

**BOOK
PUBLISHERS**
KENNEBUNKPORT, MAINE

"Where Good Books Are Ready for Press"

Visit us online at
cidermillpress.com
or write to us at
PO Box 454
12 Spring St.
Kennebunkport, Maine 04046